WOMEN'S WORLD CUP
**FRANCE
2019**
FIFA TM

KIDS' HANDBOOK

© FIFA TM

Published under licence by Carlton Books Limited
© 2019 Carlton Books Limited, 20 Mortimer Street, London W1T 3JW

ISBN 978-1-78312-449-7
10 9 8 7 6 5 4 3 2 1
Printed in Dubai

Writer: Emily Stead
Design: RockJaw Creative
Consultant: Anthony Hobbs
Kit illustrations: Peter Liddiard

The publishers would like to thank the following sources for their kind permission to reproduce the pictures in this book.

ALL PHOTOGRAPHY © GETTY IMAGES: /Action Foto Sport/NurPhoto: 35BL;
/Robin Alam/Icon Sportswire: 22R, 27R, 39TR; /Matthew Ashton-AMA: 28L;
/Lars Baron/Bongarts: 9; /Lars Baron/FIFA: 12T, 14L; /Robbie Jay Barratt-AMA:
34TR; /Daniel Bartel/Icon Sportswire: 39BL; /Angelo Blankespoor/Soccrates:
26R; /Manuel Blondeau/Icon Sport: 23L; /Simon Bruty/Sports Illustrated: 4L;
/Robert Cianflone/FIFA: 15B; /Pascal Della Zuana/Icon Sport: 23R; /Elsa: 34BL;
/Stuart Franklin/FIFA: 13T, 18, 33TR; /Laurence Griffiths: 17; /Alex Grimm: 19T;
/Dennis Grombkowski: 14BR; /Scott Heavey: 19B; /Karina Hessland: 22L; /Mike Hewitt/
FIFA: 11B, 21B; /Hagen Hopkins: 24R; /Catherine Ivill: 10; /Zak Kaczmarek: 32BL;
/Steven Kingsman/Icon Sports Wire: 12B; /Jan Kruger/UEFA: 16; /Francois
Laplante/FreestylePhoto: 13B; /Christopher Lee/UEFA: 24L, 25L; /Robert
Martinez: 20; /Maddie Meyer/FIFA: 7, 11T; /Vincent Michel/Icon Sport: 4-5, 26L,
30TR; /Jean-Francois Monier/AFP: 30BL; /Christopher Morris/Corbis: 15T; /Dan
Mullan: 35TR; /Nathan Munkley/Action Plus: 25R; /Francois Nel: 29L, 32TR; /
Adam Pulicicchio: 36BL; /Vaughn Ridley/Bongarts: 36TR, 31BL; /Lars Ronbog/
FrontZoneSport: 38BL; /Alan Smith/Icon Sportswire: 33BL; /Patrik
Stollarz/AFP: 21TR; /TF-Images: 31TR; /VI Images: 29R, 38TR; /Eric
Verhoeven/Soccrates: 27L, 37TR, 37BL; /Tim Warner: 41; /Dave
Winter/Icon Sport: 28R; /Scott Winters/Icon Sportswire: 40

FRANCE
2019

© FIFA TM

Contents

NOTE TO READER
The facts and records in this book are accurate as of 1 December 2018.

Bienvenue en France!

The FIFA Women's World Cup 2019™ will be the eighth edition of the tournament and is set to be the most-watched and most action-packed competition in the history of women's football! This handbook is your guide to the tournament – it's crammed with facts, stats, activities and fill-ins to record all the action.

Which countries are playing?

While 144 teams from six confederations around the world attempted to qualify, just 24 countries will compete for the FIFA Women's World Cup Trophy in France. France qualified automatically as the host nation, while China, Brazil and former winners Japan were among the next teams to secure their spots.

Where will the matches be played?

Nine different cities across France will host the tournament – Rennes, Paris, Le Havre, Valenciennes, Reims, Lyon, Grenoble, Nice and Montpellier. The final will be held at the Stade de Lyon on Sunday 7 July.

▲ Champions the USA are hoping to defend their crown. Scotland, Jamaica and Chile will make their first-ever appearances at the tournament.

▶ France take on Canada in a friendly in 2018. The hosts promise to put on an action-packed tournament in front of record crowds.

Fantastic FIFA Women's World Cup™ facts

Here are some awesome facts about the FIFA Women's World Cup to wow your friends and family.

Fifty-two matches will be played at France 2019, with the opener in the French capital, Paris. That means at least **4,680 minutes** of football, plus extra time!

The **FIFA Women's World Cup Trophy** was designed for the 1999 tournament. A spiral band made of bronze covered in gold encircles an aluminium football at the top. The trophy is 47cm high and weighs 4.6kg.

Women had to wait **61 years** after the first men's FIFA World Cup™ in 1930 to play in the first women's tournament.

Canada 2015 was the best-attended FIFA Women's World Cup in history, with over **1.3 million fans** going to watch the matches.

Although Germany and the USA have won **five titles** between them, they have never met in a FIFA Women's World Cup final.

The USA were the **first team** to take home the trophy following their victory at China 1991.

Switzerland's Fabienne Humm scored the fastest hat-trick in the tournament's history – it took her just **five minutes** in 2015!

MEET

ettie™ is a young chicken with a passion for life and football! She is also the mascot for the FIFA Women's World Cup 2019. Cheeky and friendly, her name comes from the French word for "star": "*étoile*". Kitted out in her country's colours – a red-and-blue stripy top – ettie™ is set to light up the tournament with her warmth and slick skills!

© FIFA TM

FEARSOME FOUR

Just four different teams have won the FIFA Women's World Cup. Rearrange the letters to work out the winners, then match the teams to their flags.

1. **PAJNA**

   Japan

2. **TUNDEI EATSTS**

   United States

3. **WRANYO**

   Norway

4. **MERYGAN**

   Germany

MISSING MATCH BALL

The 2015 tournament decider between the USA and Japan was the highest-scoring FIFA Women's World Cup final ever! Which ball is the correct one: A, B, C or D?

My FIFA Women's World Cup 2019™

The hottest tournament of 2019 kicks off on 7 June! Which international team will you be cheering on? Colour in your team's kit, then predict which teams and players will prove to be world-beaters.

The team I'm supporting: _Canada_

My favourite players: _Sam Kerr, Christine Sinclair, Alex Morgan, Mallory Pugh._

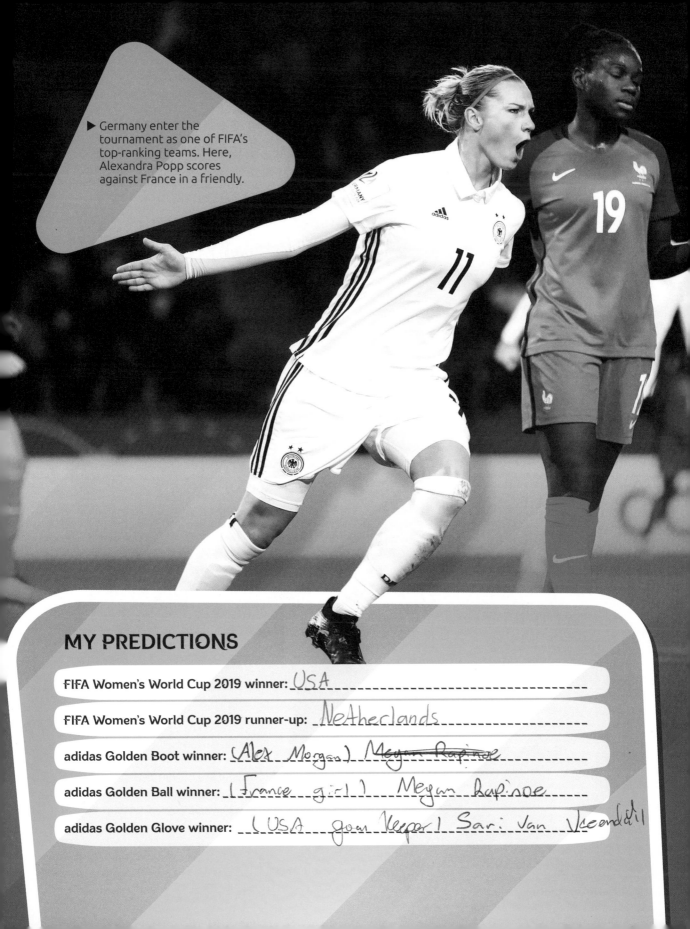

▶ Germany enter the tournament as one of FIFA's top-ranking teams. Here, Alexandra Popp scores against France in a friendly.

MY PREDICTIONS

FIFA Women's World Cup 2019 winner: USA

FIFA Women's World Cup 2019 runner-up: Netherlands

adidas Golden Boot winner: (Alex Morgan) Megan Rapinoe

adidas Golden Ball winner: (France girl) Megan Rapinoe

adidas Golden Glove winner: (USA goal keeper) Sari van Veendaal

Road to Lyon

Once all 24 spots at the FIFA Women's World Cup France 2019™ had been filled, the teams were sorted into groups in December 2018. Now each team must be at the top of its game in the month-long battle to win the ultimate prize in women's football! Here's how the tournament will play out in France, from the first round to the final.

GROUP STAGES

There are six groups made up of four teams. Each team has to play the others in its group once, with the top two teams in each group progressing to the next round. The four best third-placed teams from the six groups advance to the knockout stage as well. Goal difference could be key here.

◀ England's Toni Duggan will be hoping to open her FIFA Women's World Cup goalscoring account in France.

ROUND OF 16

The six group winners, the six runners-up and the four best third-placed teams from the groups go through to the knockout stage. In these rounds, if the scores are level after 90 minutes, 30 minutes of extra time are played. If the teams are still drawing at the end of extra time, a penalty shoot-out decides the winner.

▼ Japan advance to the semis at Canada 2015 with a narrow win over Australia in the quarter-finals.

QUARTER-FINALS

Next up are the quarter-finals, through which eight teams become four. Matches are played over 90 minutes, with extra time and penalties if needed. Germany sneaked through to the semi-finals at Canada 2015 by beating France in a penalty shoot-out. The four ties will be played in Valenciennes, Le Havre, Rennes and Paris.

SEMI-FINALS

The two semi-finals are usually nail-biting occasions, where just a single goal can decide whether a team reaches the final. The USA have made it to the semi-finals at every single edition of the tournament. Both semi-finals will be played at the 58,000-capacity Stade de Lyon.

▼ Carli Lloyd smashes home the first of the USA's five goals in the 2015 final.

The USA's 5-2 victory over Japan in the 2015 final was watched by **26.7 million viewers** in the US – a record at the time for any football game, men's or women's.

FINAL

The biggest match in women's football is the FIFA Women's World Cup final. The title has twice been decided on penalties, with the USA and Japan winning dramatic shoot-outs in 1999 and 2011 respectively, while the final at Canada 2015 was a seven-goal thriller! The Stade de Lyon will host this mega match.

Tournament rules

The referee is in charge of the game and has two assistant referees to help apply the rules. With so much to play for, referees also have state-of-the-art technology to help them do their job. Making sure that the game is played fairly is a real team effort!

▼ The refereeing team from the third-place play-off at Canada 2015 pose for a photo.

GOAL-LINE TECHNOLOGY

Goal-line technology (GLT) is a computerised camera system that monitors both goals, alerting the referee if the whole of the ball crosses the line. The difference between scoring and not scoring can be just millimetres! GLT was first introduced at the FIFA Women's World Cup™ for the 2015 tournament in Canada.

▶ At Canada 2015, Norway's goal in their 2-1 round-of-16 defeat to England was confirmed by GLT. The system was used eight times during the tournament.

VANISHING SPRAY

When a team is awarded a free kick, the referee may use a special vanishing foam spray to draw a line on the pitch, marking where opponents must stand as the free kick is taken (at least 9.15m behind the ball). Clever stuff!

◀ Vanishing spray was introduced to speed up the game. The marks on the pitch disappear after about a minute.

© FIFA TM

PICKING A WINNER

What happens if the scores are level at the end of the game?

Extra time

From the round of 16 on, matches that are drawn after 90 minutes will go into extra time. Teams must play two extra halves of 15 minutes, plus any stoppage time. If the scores are still level after 120 minutes, the match will be settled by a penalty shoot-out.

Penalty shoot-out

The FIFA Women's World Cup final has twice been decided by a penalty shoot-out, in 1999 and 2011. In a shoot-out, each team takes five penalties in turn. If the scores are still tied after five penalties each, the spot kicks go to sudden death until one team is declared the winner.

▼ The German players celebrate after beating France in a tense shoot-out in the quarter-finals at Canada 2015.

Player prizes

While the top prize for teams is the FIFA Women's World Cup™ Trophy, a host of awards are presented to the tournament's best individual performers.

adidas GOLDEN BOOT

The adidas Golden Boot is the prize every striker dreams of! It is given to the top goalscorer at the FIFA Women's World Cup and has been won by players from the USA, Norway, China, Brazil, Germany and Japan. American forward Michelle Akers hit ten goals at China 1991 and holds the record for the most goals scored in a single edition of the tournament.

◄ Former Germany striker Célia Šašić won the adidas Golden Boot in 2015, with six goals.

adidas GOLDEN BALL

This award is presented to the best player at each FIFA Women's World Cup to reward outstanding individual performances. American Carli Lloyd took home the award at Canada 2015. Only two European players have won the award – Norway's Hege Riise and Birgit Prinz of Germany.

▶ Carli Lloyd is one of women's football's outstanding players.

adidas GOLDEN GLOVE

This prize, as you may have guessed, is awarded to the tournament's best goalkeeper. Technical brilliance and clean sheets are noted by the judges. Goalkeepers can also be considered for the Golden Ball. Former USA keeper Hope Solo twice won the Golden Glove – at Germany 2011 and Canada 2015.

▲ Stopper Hope Solo played an awesome 202 games for the USA.

FIFA YOUNG PLAYER AWARD

Players aged 21 or under have a chance to be voted the best young player of the tournament. Aussie starlet Caitlin Foord was crowned the best young player at Germany 2011, aged just 16, while Canadian Kadeisha Buchanan won the trophy on home soil four years later.

◄ Caitlin Foord now has over 60 caps for the *Matildas*.

FIFA FAIR PLAY AWARD

This award is given to the team with the best record of fair play during the tournament, which could mean committing the fewest fouls or receiving the fewest yellow or red cards. Only teams that qualify for the knockout rounds are considered.

Super stadiums

Matches at the FIFA Women's World Cup 2019™ will be played in nine different cities, giving fans from all over France a taste of the action. Read about all nine great grounds.

◄ The Stade de Nice hosted France v Brazil in a warm-up match in November 2018. France won 3-1.

Stade de Nice
City: Nice
Capacity: 36,178
Matches: Four group games, round of 16, third-place play-off
Stadium stat: The stadium cost around €250 million and opened in 2013.

Stade de la Mosson
City: Montpellier
Capacity: 27,310
Matches: Four group games, round of 16
Stadium stat: The stadium hosted games during the 1998 FIFA World Cup™ men's tournament.

Stade Auguste-Delaune
City: Reims
Capacity: 19,465
Matches: Five group games, round of 16
Stadium stat: It is one of the most historic stadiums in the tournament. It hosted matches at the 1938 FIFA World Cup™!

© FIFA TM

Stade Océane
City: Le Havre
Capacity: 25,278
Matches: Five group games, round of 16, quarter-final
Stadium stat: Home to Le Havre AC, the stadium opened its doors in 2012.

Stade des Alpes
City: Grenoble
Capacity: 20,068
Matches: Four group games, round of 16
Stadium stat: The French Women's Cup final was held here in 2016.

Parc des Princes
City: Paris
Capacity: 48,583
Matches: Five group games, round of 16, quarter-final
Stadium stat: This grand ground in southwest Paris first opened back in 1897.

Roazhon Park
City: Rennes
Capacity: 29,820
Matches: Five group games, round of 16, quarter-final
Stadium stat: *Les Bleues* have appeared at the stadium three times.

Stade de Lyon
City: Lyon
Capacity: 58,215
Matches: Both semi-finals, plus the final
Stadium stat: The ground is also known as the Stadium of Lights.

Stade du Hainaut
City: Valenciennes
Capacity: 25,172
Matches: Four group games, round of 16, quarter-final
Stadium stat: Located near the Belgian border, Valenciennes FC play their football here.

▼ The state-of-the-art stadium in Lyon offers fans awesome views of the action.

Record-breakers

The FIFA Women's World Cup™ has excited fans in each one of its seven tournaments so far. Take a look at this countdown of ten famous facts from the finals since the first competition back in 1991.

10

One of Swedish star Lena Videkull's claims to fame is scoring the competition's fastest goal – it took her just 30 seconds from kick-off to score at China 1991!

◄ If Formiga is selected for Brazil's squad, it will be her seventh FIFA Women's World Cup.

9

Russia's Elena Danilova became the tournament's youngest scorer when she netted at the age of 16 years and 96 days in 2003...

8

...While the oldest goalscorer is Brazil's Formiga, who scored aged 37 years and 98 days at Canada 2015.

7

Japan became the first team from Asia to be crowned world champions when they won the trophy in 2011.

6

Legendary German keeper Nadine Angerer once went 622 minutes without letting in a goal – six clean sheets in a row.

5

The 2015 tournament in Canada was the highest-scoring in the competition's history, as 146 goals flew in.

4

The biggest win came in 2007, when Germany thumped Argentina 11-0, a scoreline that may never be bettered!

▶ Nadine Angerer won two FIFA Women's World Cups and five UEFA EUROs.

3

The final between the USA and China PR in 1999 saw the record attendance for a single match – 90,185 supporters crammed into the Rose Bowl stadium.

2

The *Stars and Stripes* have played the most matches at the FIFA Women's World Cup: 43, four ahead of Germany. The USA also have the best win rate, winning almost three-quarters of their games!

1

Brazil's super striker Marta has scored 15 goals over four tournaments – that's more than any other player in the history of the competition.

▶ Marta has been nicknamed *Pelé de saia* ("Pelé in a skirt").

Fantastic finals

In the seven FIFA Women's World Cup™ finals since the first women's tournament 28 years ago, there have been four different champions, seven finalists and goals galore! Take a look at how each final was won.

China 1991

USA 2-1 NORWAY
Stadium: Tianhe Stadium, Guangzhou
Attendance: 63,000

The USA were the first-ever FIFA Women's World Cup winners, as Michelle Akers scored twice to beat Norway over 90 minutes. Akers is one of the true legends of women's football.

Sweden 1995

GERMANY 0-2 NORWAY
Stadium: Råsunda Stadium, Stockholm
Attendance: 17,158

After being runners-up in 1991, Norway captured the FIFA Women's World Cup for the first – and only – time. Stars Hege Riise and Marianne Pettersen both scored to send Norway's fans wild!

USA 1999

USA 0-0 CHINA (5-4 pens)
Stadium: Rose Bowl, Pasadena
Attendance: 90,185

The USA became champions for a second time on home turf, but it took a nail-biting penalty shoot-out to win the trophy! Brandi Chastain scored the winning penalty in front of a huge crowd of over 90,000 fans.

USA 2003

GERMANY 2-1 SWEDEN
Stadium: Carson, California
Attendance: 26,137

The fourth FIFA Women's World Cup was once again hosted by the USA. An extra-time golden goal from Nia Künzer saw Germany crowned champions, as they beat Sweden 2-1.

China 2007

GERMANY 2-0 BRAZIL
Stadium: Hongkou Football Stadium, Shanghai
Attendance: 31,000

Germany won back-to-back FIFA Women's World Cups as the tournament returned to Asia for the first time since 1991. Captain Birgit Prinz and Simone Laudehr scored the goals, but it was Brazil's Marta who set the tournament alight.

▲ German skipper Birgit Prinz lifts the trophy in 2007.

Germany 2011

JAPAN 2-2 USA (3-1 pens)
Stadium: Waldstadion, Frankfurt
Attendance: 48,817

Japan became the fourth team to win the trophy and the first from Asia. A thrilling final was decided on penalties, as Japan, who had never reached a major final before, beat the favourites, the USA.

Canada 2015

USA 5-2 JAPAN
Stadium: BC Place, Vancouver
Attendance: 53,341

In a rematch of the 2011 final, the USA were determined to make up for their loss in Germany. They claimed their third FIFA Women's World Cup in emphatic fashion by scoring five goals – including four in the first 16 minutes!

▲ Japan took the title against all the odds in 2011.

◣ The USA's Abby Wambach celebrates in 2015. She has scored more international goals than any other player, male or female.

The answers are at the back of the book.

Quick quiz

Test your knowledge of the tournament finals!

1. In how many finals have the USA appeared?

a. three   b. four   c. six

2. China were the first team from Asia to win the trophy.

a. true   b. false

3. The record attendance for a final was at USA 1999. How big was the crowd?

a. 59,018   b. 18,590   c. 90,185

Cool keepers

Goalkeepers are key players for any team and the last line of defence. They need to stay switched-on for the whole 90 minutes and beyond, as plenty of FIFA Women's World Cup™ matches are decided on penalty shoot-outs. Here's a look at some of the best shot-stoppers currently on show.

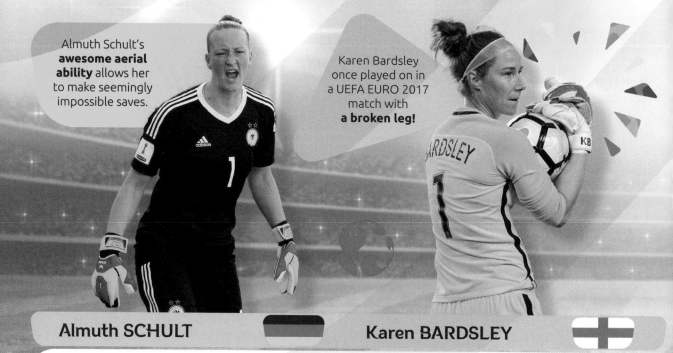

Almuth Schult's **awesome aerial ability** allows her to make seemingly impossible saves.

Karen Bardsley once played on in a UEFA EURO 2017 match with **a broken leg!**

Almuth SCHULT

COUNTRY: Germany

CLUB: Wolfsburg (German league)

BORN: 9 February 1991

CAPS: 56

Karen BARDSLEY

COUNTRY: England

CLUB: Manchester City (English league)

BORN: 14 October 1984

CAPS: 74

Tall and athletic, Schult has played over 50 games for Germany since 2011. She had big boots to fill when she started out, taking over from the legendary Nadine Angerer, but played every minute for the Germany team that won gold at the 2016 Olympics. France 2019 will be Schult's first FIFA Women's World Cup as Germany's number 1.

Bardsley was born and raised in the USA, where she also learned her trade as a goalkeeper. A tall keeper with great positional sense, she is brilliant in one-on-one situations. Bardsley has the final at France 2019 in her sights, after helping the *Three Lionesses* to a third-place finish last time around.

Hedvig Lindahl helped Sweden to a **third-place finish** at Germany 2011.

Look out for Sarah Bouhaddi in a shoot-out – she can **save and score** penalty kicks!

Hedvig LINDAHL

COUNTRY: Sweden

CLUB: Chelsea (English league)

BORN: 29 April 1983

CAPS: 153

Lindahl dreamed of becoming a goalkeeper from a young age, and is one of the world's top players in any position. She has been Sweden's best keeper since 2002 and has over 150 caps. Ice-cool when facing penalties, Lindahl's heroics helped her country to a silver medal at the 2016 Olympics, as Sweden eliminated the USA and Brazil in shoot-outs.

Sarah BOUHADDI

COUNTRY: France

CLUB: Lyon (French league)

BORN: 17 October 1986

CAPS: 134

Brilliant Bouhaddi has claimed over 100 caps for *Les Bleues*, having made her debut back in 2004 as a 17-year-old. She possesses amazing reflexes and is as comfortable with the ball at her feet as any of her outfield team-mates. Playing in her second FIFA Women's World Cup, Bouhaddi will be a contender for the adidas Golden Glove.

Dynamite defenders

No team has ever won the FIFA Women's World Cup™ without a strong defence. These players work tirelessly while supporting the team in attacking free kicks and corners too. Here are four defenders who have got the lot!

PSG's Irene Paredes is one of Europe's **top centre-backs**.

Cool Saki Kumagai **leads by example**.

Irene PAREDES

COUNTRY: Spain

CLUB: Paris Saint-Germain (French league)

BORN: 4 July 1991

CAPS: 55

GOALS: 8

One of Spain's standout stars, central defender Paredes is comfortable playing the ball out from the back and likes to join the attack, too: she's scored eight international goals so far! Her first cap came in 2011 and Paredes has represented Spain at two UEFA EUROs and one FIFA Women's World Cup.

Saki KUMAGAI

COUNTRY: Japan

CLUB: Lyon (French league)

BORN: 17 October 1990

CAPS: 100

GOALS: 0

Japan's skipper plays in defence for her country, but features in midfield for Lyon, where she is often on the scoresheet. She is great at breaking up attacking moves and has a strong will to win. Kumagai's career highlight was when she scored the winning penalty as Japan beat the USA to clinch the FIFA Women's World Cup in 2011.

Lucy Bronze is one of the **driving forces** behind England.

Nilla Fischer was first selected for Sweden as a **16-year-old**.

Nilla FISCHER

COUNTRY: Sweden

CLUB: Wolfsburg (German league)

BORN: 2 August 1984

CAPS: 171

GOALS: 23

Centre-back Nilla Fischer is a tremendous tackler with years of experience for her national side, Sweden. She made her international debut in 2001 and has won many caps for her country as a defensive midfielder. If Fischer is selected for the squad, France 2019 will be her fourth FIFA Women's World Cup finals.

Lucy BRONZE

COUNTRY: England

CLUB: Lyon (French league)

BORN: 28 October 1991

CAPS: 62

GOALS: 7

Brilliant Bronze is considered by many people to be the best right-back in the world. Strong and quick, she is an intelligent player who reads the game well. She is also known for popping up with goals at key moments, and scored one of the goals of the tournament at Canada 2015 – a cracking right-foot shot from distance. World class!

Mega midfielders

Midfielders are often called the "engine" of the team. They do loads of running and must support the defence and the attack. This quality quartet can link the play and score goals themselves – important skills for midfielders.

Amandine Henry was first given the **captain's armband** for *Les Bleues* in 2017.

Izzy Christiansen could have chosen to **play for Denmark**, but began training with England as a teenager.

Amandine HENRY

COUNTRY: France

CLUB: Lyon (French league)

BORN: 28 September 1989

CAPS: 78

GOALS: 11

France's Henry is among the best central midfielders in the world but shines in a number of positions. She made her international debut a decade ago and her tournament experience will be all-important at France 2019. Henry's awesome displays at Canada 2015 won her the adidas Silver Ball award, behind Carli Lloyd.

Izzy CHRISTIANSEN

COUNTRY: England

CLUB: Lyon (French league)

BORN: 20 September 1991

CAPS: 28

GOALS: 6

Christiansen brings creativity and goals to England's midfield, while working hard for the team. She made her debut for the national side against Estonia in 2015, opening her goalscoring account in the same game. She was a member of the *Three Lionesses'* squad at UEFA EURO 2017, and France 2019 will be her first FIFA Women's World Cup™.

Experienced Megan Rapinoe still has **plenty to contribute** to her national side.

Lieke Martens scored her **first FIFA Women's World Cup goal** against New Zealand in 2015.

Lieke MARTENS

COUNTRY: Netherlands

CLUB: Barcelona (Spanish league)

BORN: 16 December 1992

CAPS: 97

GOALS: 40

A key member of the Dutch team, Martens is a skilful, quick and direct winger with a "goal-den" touch – she has scored close to 50 international goals at all levels. Martens was named player of the tournament at UEFA EURO 2017, inspiring the Netherlands to glory. Despite being right-footed, Martens prefers to play on the left flank.

Megan RAPINOE

COUNTRY: USA

CLUB: Seattle Reign (US league)

BORN: 5 July 1985

CAPS: 145

GOALS: 41

Anything can happen when midfield star Rapinoe has the ball at her feet! She can create goals, score them and shoot with both feet. She has overcome two serious injuries in her career to play over 140 times for the *Stars and Stripes*, and has featured in two FIFA Women's World Cup finals, lifting the trophy in 2015. She is a true US legend!

Flying forwards

Meet four goal machines from around the world who have the skills, pace and power to devastate defences in France! Who will you back to be the tournament's top scorer in the race for the adidas Golden Boot?

Marta's full name is **Marta Vieira da Silva**.

Eugénie Le Sommer is France's **second-highest goalscorer** of all time.

MARTA 🇧🇷

COUNTRY: Brazil

CLUB: Orlando Pride (US league)

BORN: 19 February 1986

CAPS: 133

GOALS: 110

One of the best female footballers ever, Marta has scored more than 100 times for Brazil and is the all-time FIFA Women's World Cup™ top scorer with 15 goals. This hotshot striker is so good that she was named FIFA Women's Player of the Year five times in a row! Now in her 30s, France 2019 is likely to be her final FIFA Women's World Cup.

Eugénie LE SOMMER 🇫🇷

COUNTRY: France

CLUB: Lyon (French league)

BORN: 18 May 1989

CAPS: 156

GOALS: 73

One of the most talented strikers in the world, Eugénie Le Sommer can light up any game. She is great at powering past defenders and has a magical eye for goal. She has played for *Les Bleues* for over a decade, having made her debut as a teenager. France 2019 will be her third FIFA Women's World Cup.

Vivianne Miedema will be **just 22** when France 2019 kicks off.

Sam Kerr scored **11 goals in 14 games** for **Australia** from September 2017 to April 2018.

Sam KERR

COUNTRY: Australia

CLUB: Chicago Red Stars (US league)

BORN: 10 September 1993

CAPS: 72

GOALS: 27

With blistering pace and lethal finishing, awesome Australian striker Kerr could be one of the most dangerous players in France. She was just 15 when she made her full international debut, and she helped Australia to claim the Tournament of Nations in 2017. Look out for her back-flipping goal celebration at the FIFA Women's World Cup France 2019!

Vivianne MIEDEMA

COUNTRY: Netherlands

CLUB: Arsenal (English league)

BORN: 15 July 1996

CAPS: 68

GOALS: 53

Dazzling Dutch striker Vivianne Miedema exploded onto the international scene in 2013 as a teenager and has not stopped scoring since! Her ability to shoot with either foot as well as her clinical finishing should see Miedema open her goalscoring account on the global stage in her second FIFA Women's World Cup.

France

As the host nation, France qualified for their fourth FIFA Women's World Cup™ automatically. The team combines experienced defenders with a youthful attack. France lost to Germany on penalties in the quarter-finals at Canada 2015, so now *Les Bleues* will be looking to go further this year and take the title on home turf.

NICKNAME: *Les Bleues* ("the Blues")
COACH: Corinne Diacre
CAPTAIN: Amandine Henry
MOST CAPS: Sandrine Soubeyrand (198)
TOP SCORER: Marinette Pichon (81)
PREVIOUS APPEARANCES: 3
BEST FINISH: 4th place (2011)

ONE TO WATCH

Towering centre-back Wendie Renard **is one of the first names on the French team sheet. Playing in her third FIFA Women's World Cup,** this tough-tackling and sure-footed defender is one of the most experienced stoppers in women's football.

◀ France have only once gone beyond the quarter-finals at a FIFA Women's World Cup.

Germany

Germany are always among the favourites at any major tournament, having been crowned FIFA Women's World Cup winners in 2003 and 2007 and European champions eight times. They reached the semi-finals in 2015, and new manager Martina Voss-Tecklenburg will be hoping to go one round further this time.

NICKNAME: *Die Nationalelf* ("the National Eleven")
COACH: Martina Voss-Tecklenburg
CAPTAIN: Dzsenifer Marozsán
MOST CAPS: Birgit Prinz (214)
TOP SCORER: Birgit Prinz (128)
PREVIOUS APPEARANCES: 7
BEST FINISH: Champions (2003, 2007)

ONE TO WATCH

Midfielder Dzsenifer Marozsán **is brilliant at linking attack and defence, and was given the captain's armband for Germany in October 2016. France 2019 will be her second FIFA Women's World Cup.**

◀ In UEFA qualifying Group 5, Germany recorded an astonishing 11-0 win over the Faroe Islands.

Australia

After missing out on the very first FIFA Women's World Cup™, Australia have qualified for every edition since. They have reached the quarter-finals three times and rank among FIFA's top ten teams in the world. The *Matildas* head to France following a strong qualifying campaign.

NICKNAME: The *Matildas*
COACH: Alen Stajcic
CAPTAINS: Lisa De Vanna and Clare Polkinghorne
MOST CAPS: Cheryl Salisbury (151)
TOP SCORER: Lisa De Vanna (45)
PREVIOUS APPEARANCES: 6
BEST FINISH: Quarter-finals (2007, 2011, 2015)

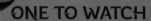

ONE TO WATCH

Nicknamed *Mini*, Katrina Gorry **is a dynamic playmaker with plenty of pace. She loves to shoot from distance and catch the goalkeeper off guard. Gorry's big-game experience will be important if the** *Matildas* **are to reach the knockout stages at France 2019.**

◀ The Australians head to France 2019 boasting their strongest-ever squad.

Brazil

Brazil have appeared at every FIFA Women's World Cup so far, yet they have never been crowned champions. They have players who are capable of chipping in with goals from every area of the pitch, as well as plenty of experienced heads. Coach Vadão leads his team to the FIFA Women's World Cup finals for the second time.

NICKNAME: *A Seleção* ("the National Squad")
COACH: Oswaldo Alvarez (Vadão)
CAPTAIN: Marta
MOST CAPS: Formiga (170)
TOP SCORER: Marta (110)
PREVIOUS APPEARANCES: 7
BEST FINISH: Runners-up (2007)

ONE TO WATCH

Forward **Débora Cristiane de Oliveira**, known as Debinha, has played her football all over the world – from Brazil to Norway to the USA. Having missed out on the 2011 and 2015 tournaments, she is hoping to form a deadly strike partnership with Marta in France.

◀ Brazil's squad is studded with samba stars!

33

Japan

Winners of the trophy in 2011, Japan are aiming to reach their third FIFA Women's World Cup™ final in a row. Their squad is one of the youngest in the tournament, with only a couple of players over the age of 30. They are the only Asian side to be crowned world champions, but lost out to the USA in the 2015 final.

NICKNAME: *Nadeshiko* (a pink mountain flower)
COACH: Asako Takakura
CAPTAIN: Saki Kumagai
MOST CAPS: Homare Sawa (205)
TOP SCORER: Homare Sawa (83)
PREVIOUS APPEARANCES: 7
BEST FINISH: Champions (2011)

ONE TO WATCH

Forward Mana Iwabuchi was a FIFA Women's World Cup winner two tournaments ago. She is a pacy attacker who has played more than 60 times for Japan, scoring over 20 goals. The Tokyo-born player is a real danger to defences.

◀ Japan have a point to prove after losing the last FIFA Women's World Cup final 5-2 to the USA.

England

England have played at four FIFA Women's World Cups and stormed to their highest finish at Canada 2015, beating Germany in the play-off for third place. Under manager Phil Neville, a team that includes world-class stars such as Lucy Bronze, Steph Houghton and Fran Kirby could go far in France.

NICKNAME: The *Three Lionesses*
COACH: Phil Neville
CAPTAIN: Steph Houghton
MOST CAPS: Fara Williams (170)
TOP SCORER: Kelly Smith (46)
PREVIOUS APPEARANCES: 4
BEST FINISH: 3rd place (2015)

ONE TO WATCH

All-round attacker Toni Duggan **is strong with both feet and has a great goalscoring record for her country. Duggan plays her club football for Barcelona and has won over 60 international caps.**

◄ Ace defender Steph Houghton (top row, third from left) has captained the side since 2014.

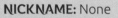 Canada

Hosts of the previous tournament in 2015, Canada's incredible progress in recent years has seen them earn a FIFA ranking among the top teams in the world. Their squad blends experienced heads with teenage talent and the side now boasts flair players as well as a solid defence.

NICKNAME: None
COACH: Kenneth Heiner-Møller
CAPTAIN: Christine Sinclair
MOST CAPS: Christine Sinclair (274)
TOP SCORER: Christine Sinclair (177)
PREVIOUS APPEARANCES: 6
BEST FINISH: 4th place (2003)

ONE TO WATCH

Forward Christine Sinclair is unstoppable, even aged 35! With a natural eye for goal, Sinclair has netted over 170 times for Canada. Her tournament goal haul stands at an impressive nine goals over four FIFA Women's World Cup™ tournaments – could she reach double figures at France 2019?

◀ Canada will be aiming to reach the final for the first time in France.

Netherlands

Appearing at only their second FIFA Women's World Cup, the Netherlands are ranked in the world's top ten teams. They won their first major women's trophy at UEFA EURO 2017, beating Denmark 4-2. With prolific goalscorers Lieke Martens and Vivianne Miedema in the side, the squad could go all the way.

NICKNAME: *De Leeuwinnen* ("the Lionesses")
COACH: Sarina Wiegman
CAPTAIN: Anouk Dekker
MOST CAPS: Annemieke Kiesel (156)
TOP SCORER: Manon Melis (59)
PREVIOUS APPEARANCES: 1
BEST FINISH: Round of 16 (2015)

ONE TO WATCH

Daniëlle van de Donk **is a dynamo in midfield, playing in an attacking role for the Dutch. Comfortable on the ball, she is a tough tackler who can also deliver a killer pass. She will be a key player for the Netherlands in France.**

◀ The Netherlands were the last European team to qualify, after beating Switzerland 4-1 in the play-off final.

Sweden

Sweden are one of the few teams to have played in every FIFA Women's World Cup™. They have come close to winning the trophy, finishing as runners-up to Germany in 2003. Experienced attacker Kosovare Asllani is the side's current leading scorer.

NICKNAME: *Blågult* (the "Blue and Yellows")
COACH: Peter Gerhardsson
CAPTAIN: Caroline Seger
MOST CAPS: Therese Sjögran (214)
TOP SCORER: Lotta Schelin (88)
PREVIOUS APPEARANCES: 7
BEST FINISH: Runners-up (2003)

ONE TO WATCH

A hard-working midfielder, Caroline Seger **made her international debut in 2005 and has won over a century of international caps.** Seger has previously captained Sweden at two FIFA Women's World Cups.

◀ Sweden will be outsiders to win the title at France 2019.

USA

Three-time world champions, the USA are always among the favourites at any FIFA Women's World Cup. Experienced stars such as co-captains Carli Lloyd and Alex Morgan will be desperate to win back-to-back world titles for the first time. Could 2019 be the year that the *Stars and Stripes* defend their crown?

NICKNAME: The *Stars and Stripes*
COACH: Jill Ellis
CAPTAINS: Carli Lloyd, Alex Morgan and Megan Rapinoe
MOST CAPS: Kristine Lilly (354)
TOP SCORER: Abby Wambach (184)
PREVIOUS APPEARANCES: 7
BEST FINISH: Champions (1991, 1999, 2015)

ONE TO WATCH

Tobin Heath **shines from wide positions. Best known for her dribbling and technical ability, her pinpoint crosses have earned her over 140 caps for the USA over a decade. If the winger is selected, France 2019 will be her third FIFA Women's World Cup.**

◀ Will the USA extend their record by storming to their fourth title in France?

Tournament teasers

Tackle these activities and puzzles to find out whether you are a world-class player!

© FIFA TM

The answers are at the back of the book.

Picture puzzler

Circle eight differences between these matchday pictures showing Australia and Brazil in action!

Superstars and stripes

Put this picture back in order to reveal a superstar of women's football.

Order:

◯ ◯ ◯ ◯

The player is:

Carli

Lloyd

A   B   C   D

FIFA Women's World Cup™ word search

Look for the names of 15 stars hiding in the grid below.
All are hoping to shine at France 2019!

```
P Y Z S X S D M P W K M F N B
E R T P Q J A Y P O J T U H L
M N M D L R E G O E P Y G B I
O E B R O N Z E L L O P Z A A
R H V Z C U F D N S L I G H D
G Q S S K K E F A T R A M U W
A A K E R R B L X I M L E J M
N V S X O X A P X U U X T D A
S N E T R A M L K R H E B Y O
D V A U H A J G H X N O U I S
J V P F Y I T G Y A W V U K O
H E Y Q A B R J O A D B L D M
F B B R M X X D K Y V N P H R
L T O F K D W B Q S V H I P E
B H U I T E M A Z R J I J L H
```

 MAROZSÁN   MARTENS   POPP

MARTA   MORGAN   LLOYD

BRONZE   KUMAGAI   MJELDE

HUITEMA   HENRY   SO-YUN

KERR   LINDAHL   HERMOSO

The group stage

Fill in the scores after each match has been played. When the groups have been decided, complete the tables. Which teams will progress to the knockout stage?

GROUP A

Date	Home			Away	Venue
7 June, 21:00	**France**	4	0	Korea Rep.	Paris
8 June, 21:00	**Norway**	3	0	Nigeria	Reims
12 June, 15:00	**Nigeria**	2	0	Korea Rep.	Grenoble
12 June, 21:00	**France**	2	1	Norway	Nice
17 June, 21:00	**Nigeria**	0	1	France	Rennes
17 June, 21:00	**Korea Rep.**	1	2	Norway	Reims

GROUP A table

TEAM	W	D	L	GD	Pts
France	3	0	0	6	9
Norway	2	0	1	3	4
Nigeria	1	0	2	-2	4
South Korea	0	0	3	-7	0

GROUP B

Date	Home			Away	Venue
8 June, 15:00	**Germany**	1	0	China PR	Rennes
8 June, 18:00	**Spain**	3	1	South Africa	Le Havre
12 June, 18:00	**Germany**	1	0	Spain	Valenciennes
13 June, 21:00	**South Africa**	0	1	China PR	Paris
17 June, 18:00	**China PR**	0	0	Spain	Le Havre
17 June, 18:00	**South Africa**	0	4	Germany	Montpellier

GROUP B table

TEAM	W	D	L	GD	Pts
Germany	3	0	0	6	
Spain	1	1	1		
China PR	1	1	1	-0	
South Africa	0	0	3	-7	

GROUP C

Date	Home			Away	Venue
9 June, 13:00	**Australia**	1	2	Italy	Valenciennes
9 June, 15:30	**Brazil**	3	0	Jamaica	Grenoble
13 June, 18:00	**Australia**	3	2	Brazil	Montpellier
14 June, 18:00	**Jamaica**	0	5	Italy	Reims
18 June, 21:00	**Italy**	0	1	Brazil	Valenciennes
18 June, 21:00	**Jamaica**	1	4	Australia	Grenoble

GROUP C table

TEAM	W	D	L	GD	Pts
Italy	2	0	1	5	6
Australia	2	0	1	3	6
Brazil	2	0	1	3	6
Jamaica	0	0	3	-11	0

GROUP D

Date						Venue
9 June, 18:00	**England**	2	1	**Scotland**		Nice
10 June, 18:00	**Argentina**	0	0	**Japan**		Paris
14 June, 15:00	**Japan**	2	1	**Scotland**		Rennes
14 June, 21:00	**England**	1	0	**Argentina**		Le Havre
19 June, 21:00	**Scotland**	3	3	**Argentina**		Paris
19 June, 21:00	**Japan**	0	2	**England**		Nice

GROUP D table

TEAM	W	D	L	GD	Pts
England	3	0	0	4	9
Japan	1	1	1	-1	4
Argentina	0	2	1	-1	2
Scotland	0	1	2	-2	1

GROUP E

Date						Venue
10 June, 21:00	**Canada**	1	0	**Cameroon**		Montpellier
11 June, 15:00	**New Zealand**	0	1	**Netherlands**		Le Havre
15 June, 15:00	**Netherlands**	3	1	**Cameroon**		Valenciennes
15 June, 21:00	**Canada**	2	0	**New Zealand**		Grenoble
20 June, 18:00	**Netherlands**	2	1	**Canada**		Reims
20 June, 18:00	**Cameroon**	2	1	**New Zealand**		Montpellier

GROUP E table

TEAM	W	D	L	GD	Pts
Netherlands	3	0	0	4	9
Canada	2	0	1	2	6
Cameroon	1	0	2	-2	3
New Zealand	0	0	3	-4	0

GROUP F

Date						Venue
11 June, 18:00	**Chile**	0	2	**Sweden**		Rennes
11 June, 21:00	**USA**	13	0	**Thailand**		Reims
16 June, 15:00	**Sweden**	5	1	**Thailand**		Nice
16 June, 18:00	**USA**	3	0	**Chile**		Paris
20 June, 21:00	**Sweden**	0	2	**USA**		Le Havre
20 June, 21:00	**Thailand**	0	2	**Chile**		Rennes

GROUP F table

TEAM	W	D	L	GD	Pts
USA	3	0	0	18	9
Sweden	2	0	1	4	6
Chile	1	0	2	-3	3
Thailand	0	0	3	-19	0

Note: All times are local times (CET).

Round of 16

Eight teams have headed home, and now the remaining 16 must win over 90 minutes or they face extra time and maybe even a penalty shoot-out.

22 June, 17:30
GRENOBLE

Spain	1	2	USA

Goalscorers: | **Goalscorers:**

Jennifer Hermoso 9 | Megan Rapinoe 7

| Megan Rapinoe 16 P

Cards: | **Cards:**

Yellow 1 | yellow 1

Player of the match:
Megan Rapinoe

22 June, 21:00
↑ NICE ↖

Norway	4	1	Austrailia

Goalscorers: | **Goalscorers:**

Yellow 3 |

| red 1

Cards: | **Cards:**

Isabell Herlovsen 31 | Elise Kellond Knight 83

Player of the match:
Caroline graham Hansen

23 June, 17:30
VALENCIENNES

England	3	0	Cameroon

Goalscorers: | **Goalscorers:**

Steph Houton 14
Ellen white 45+4
Alex Greenwood 58 |

Cards: | **Cards:**

| Yellow 2

Player of the match:
Steph Houghton

23 June, 21:00
LE HAVRE

France	2	1	Brazil

Goalscorers: | **Goalscorers:**

Valérie Gauvin 52
Amandine Henry 106 | Thaisa 63

Cards: | **Cards:**

Yellow 1 | Jellow 4

Player of the match:
Amandine Henry

WOMEN'S WORLD CUP FRANCE 2019

24 June, 18:00
REIMS

| Italy | 2 | 0 | China |

Goalscorers: | **Goalscorers:**

| Valentina Giacinti 15 | |
| Aurora Galli 49 | |

Cards: | **Cards:**
| 0 | | 0 |
| | |

Player of the match:
Valentina Giacinti

24 June, 21:00
PARIS

| Netherlands | 2 | 1 | Japan |

Goalscorers: | **Goalscorers:**

| Lieke Martens 17 | Yui Hasegawa 43 |
| Lieke Martens 90 P | |

Cards: | **Cards:**
| Yellow 0 | yellow 1 |
| | |

Player of the match:
Lieke Martens.

25 June, 18:00
MONTPELLIER

| Germany | 3 | 0 | Nigeria |

Goalscorers: | **Goalscorers:**

Alexandra Popp 20	
Sara Däbritz 27 P	
Lea Schüller 82	

Cards: | **Cards:**
| 2 yellow | yellow 3 |
| | |

Player of the match:
Alexandra Popp

25 June, 21:00
RENNES

| Sweden | 1 | 0 | Canada |

Goalscorers: | **Goalscorers:**

| Stina Blackstenius 55 | |
| | |

Cards: | **Cards:**
| yellow 2 | yellow 1 |
| | |

Player of the match:
Hedvig Lindahl

Note: All times are local times (CET).

Quarter-finals

Eight teams battle it out in this next knockout round.

WOMEN'S WORLD CUP
FRANCE 2019
FIFA ™

27 June, 21:00
LE HAVRE

England	3	0	Norway

Goalscorers: | **Goalscorers:**

Jill Scott 3
Ellen White 40

Lucy Bronze 57

Cards: | **Cards:**

Yellow 0 | yellow 1

Player of the match:
Lucy Bronze

28 June, 21:00
PARIS

France	1	2	USA

Goalscorers: | **Goalscorers:**

Wendie Renard 81 | Megan Rapinoe 5

| Megan Rapinoe 65

Cards: | **Cards:**

2 yellow | 0 yellow

Player of the match:
Megan Rapinoe

29 June, 15:00
VALENCIENNES

Italy	0	2	Netherlands

Goalscorers: | **Goalscorers:**

| Vivianne Miedema 70

| Stefanie van der gragt 8?

Cards: | **Cards:**

4 yellow | 0 yellow

Player of the match:
Vivianne Miedema

29 June, 18:30
RENNES

Germany	1	2	Sweden

Goalscorers: | **Goalscorers:**

Lina Magull 16 | Sofia Jakobsson 22

| Stina Blacksteinus 48

Cards: | **Cards:**

0 yellow | 1 yellow

Player of the match:
Sofia Jakobsson

Note: All times are local times (CET).

Semi-finals

Only two teams can reach the tournament final,
while the losers from each tie play off to decide third place.

2 July, 21:00
LYON

England [1] [2] USA

Goalscorers: | **Goalscorers:**

Ellen White 19 | Christen Press 10
| Alex Morgan 31

Cards: | **Cards:**

yellow 1 | yellow 2
red 1 | red 0

Player of the match:
Alex Morgan

3 July, 21:00
LYON

Netherlands [1] [0] Sweden

Goalscorers: | **Goalscorers:**

Jackie Groenen 99 |

Cards: | **Cards:**

yellow 2 | yellow 1

Player of the match:
Jackie Groenen

Third-place play-off
6 July, 17:00
NICE

England [0] [2] Sweden

Goalscorers: | **Goalscorers:**

Fran Kirby 31 | Kosovare Asllani 11
| Sofia Jakobsson 22

Cards: | **Cards:**

yellow 1 | yellow 1

Player of the match:
Sofia Jakobsson

Final
7 July, 17:00
LYON

USA [2] [0] Netherlands

Goalscorers: | **Goalscorers:**

Megan Rapinoe 61 |
Rose Lavelle 69 |

Cards: | **Cards:**

yellow 1 | yellow 2

Player of the match:
Megan Rapinoe

Answers

Page 7
FEARSOME FOUR
1. Japan
2. United States
3. Norway
4. Germany

MISSING MATCH BALL
Ball A is the correct one.

Page 21
1. b – four
2. False – it was Japan in 2011.
3. c – 90,185

Pages 40–41
PICTURE PUZZLER

SUPERSTARS AND STRIPES

D   C   B   A

The player is **Carli Lloyd.**

FIFA WOMEN'S WORLD CUP™ WORD SEARCH

```
P Y Z S X S D M R W K M F N B
E R T P Q J A Y P O I T U H L
M N M D I R E G O E R Y G B I
O E B R O N Z E L L O R Z A A
R H V Z C U F D N S L I G H D
G Q S S K K E F A T R A M U W
A A K E R R B L X I M L E J M
N V S X O X A P X U U X T D A
S N E T R A M L K R H E B Y O
D V A U H A J G H X N O U I S
J V P F Y I T G Y A W V U K O
H E Y Q A B R J O A D B L D M
F B B R M X X D K V H P H R
L T O F K D W B Q S V H I P E
B H U I T E M A Z R J I J B H
```

© FIFA TM